Birds Nests

By Sunita Apte

Scott Foresman
is an imprint of

Glenview, Illinois • Boston, Massachusetts • Chandler, Arizona •
Upper Saddle River, New Jersey

Photographs

Every effort has been made to secure permission and provide appropriate credit for photographic material. The publisher deeply regrets any omission and pledges to correct errors called to its attention in subsequent editions.

Unless otherwise acknowledged, all photographs are the property of Pearson Education, Inc.

Photo locators denoted as follows: Top (T), Center (C), Bottom (B), Left (L), Right (R), Background (Bkgd)

Opener: ©bethany ebling/Alamy Images; **1** ©Daniel Dempster Photography/Alamy Images; **3** ©bethany ebling/Alamy Images; **4** ©Werner Bollmann/PhotoLibrary Group, Inc.; **5** ©Greg Vaughn/Alamy Images; **6** ©Daniel Dempster Photography/Alamy Images; **8** Jupiter Images.

ISBN 13: 978-0-328-46383-1
ISBN 10:   0-328-46383-3

A robin builds a nest
with twigs.

A weaver bird builds a
nest with grass.

An eagle builds a nest
high in a tree.

A swallow builds a nest with mud.

A flamingo also builds a nest with mud.

An owl builds a nest
in a tree trunk.